FORERUNNERS: IDEAS FIRST FROM THE UNIVERSITY OF MINNESOTA PRESS

Original e-works to spark new scholarship

FORERUNNERS: IDEAS FIRST is a thought-in-process series of break-through digital works. Written between fresh ideas and finished books, Forerunners draws on scholarly work initiated in notable blogs, social media, conference plenaries, journal articles, and the synergy of academic exchange. This is gray literature publishing: where intense thinking, change, and speculation take place in scholarship.

Ten Theses for an
Aesthetics of Politics

Ten Theses for an Aesthetics of Politics

Davide Panagia

University of Minnesota Press

MINNEAPOLIS

Published by the University of Minnesota Press, 2016
111 Third Avenue South, Suite 290
Minneapolis, MN 55401–2520
http://www.upress.umn.edu

We didn't need dialogue. We had faces.

—NORMA DESMOND in *Sunset Boulevard* (1950)

Contents

Preface

THE FIRST DRAFT of these *Ten Theses for an Aesthetics of Politics* was written some years ago. The revisions took a while. And the willingness to consider publication was prolonged. All of this is to say that I'm thrilled to have the opportunity to participate in such an exciting publishing venture as Forerunners that fosters the critical intensity of the transitory feuilleton in the digital age. What spurred my writing was a sense of dissatisfaction (palpable throughout this text) with a general contention of critical thinking: namely, that appearances are collusive to progressive politics. The reigning orthodoxy in the study of aesthetics and politics considers aesthetic objects as things about whose politics we must be skeptical. All forms of aesthetic pleasure are reducible to consumption, so it seems, and appearances seem more or less equivalent to the commercial products Madison Avenue wants us to want. One rarely speaks favorably of Hollywood film-making, or of pop music. And it is even more rare to find positive accounts of spectatorship. All of this is to say that studies in the aesthetics of politics are often—not always, but more often than not—presented in the negative, where aesthetic appreciation and distraction is something that our most heartened forms of political judgment and critical thinking must overcome. This is because, try as we might, we just can't seem to shake the epistemic intuition of our modern modes of political thinking that say appearances are deceitful and all surfaces must be plumbed so as to get at the truth of the matter.

In short, what spurred this piece of writing was a dissatisfaction with a collective common sense that imbues much contemporary political criticism: namely, that aesthetic experiences demand epistemic critique, and that critique requires a denial of aesthetic appreciation. The world of appearances, in short, is delusion all the way down.

In part my dissatisfaction with this approach stems from what I take to be a demonization of the demos. For if it is true that instances of aesthetic appreciation are akin to intellectual stultification, and if spectatorship is characterized as a space of distraction from what is properly political, then the everyday moments we all have of looking, hearing, touching, tasting, and smelling, and those minute instances whereby we derive an unverifiable sense of pleasure or disturbance from such moments of aesthetic appreciation, are simply bad. What's worse, our willingness to entertain such moments means perpetuating a pervasive evil in the world—the evil of political seduction and moral distraction. If aesthetic appreciation is unpurposive, political life must be purposive—and the two trajectories shall never meet; or, better, *must* never meet.

The experiments of thinking, of engagement, and discussion that generated the *Ten Theses for an Aesthetics of Politics* took place in undergraduate and graduate classrooms at Trent University (Canada) where I had the privilege to teach for ten years, at the University of California, Los Angeles, where I currently teach, and at various conferences, workshops, bars, restaurants, living rooms, and other sundry places and spaces with generous people provoked by the idea that maybe, just maybe, our relation to the world of appearances isn't as settled as we think it is, and that one of the ways in which we may think the aesthetics of politics is to consider not just the epistemic conditions for understanding works but the diverse forms of relations and solidarity that emerge when we attend to a world of advening appearances.

There was one other occurrence that spurred my sense of urgency about the importance of rethinking the relation of politics and aesthetics, and that is the proliferation of sites and sounds of peoples throughout the globe traversing invisible lines, seeking refuge and asylum. And it became somewhat perspicuous that the critical attitude taken toward aesthetic objects is akin to (maybe even the same as) the hesitance afforded stateless peoples who affront our visual field in the media, at airport border crossings, in everyday encounters. In all instances, the intuition is to turn away from the appearance by asking a version of the question "How do I know that she really is the way she appears to be?" How do I know that the refugee really needs asylum? Or, how do I know that the aesthetic object is what it seems to be? These two different but parallel questions offer the same hesitation: that is, a reluctance to give admittance to that which advenes; a reluctance that is buttressed by a set of demands and expectations for verification through reason-giving, for fear that without these the inherited ways of being in the world will be dislodged. Both scenarios beg a form of spectatorship and both take a knowing stance toward a perceptual field so as to stay the difficult work of be/holding.

I am taken by that moment in Stanley Cavell's writings that ponders our need to verify the truth of a sensation that can't be verified (a need he calls skepticism). Such a sensation can be a sense of beauty, or suffering, or happiness, or hunger. It describes a moment when we are captured by the appearance of something to which we can't relate. A classic formulation, the one that captures me most, is when Cavell describes film actors on a screen not as humans but as *human somethings*, because what we see on those scrims are luminosities projected by a machine that animates light fragments at twenty-four frames per second. And yet, we experience sensations vis-à-vis those human *somethings* as if they were *human* somethings. All of this is to suggest that our senses of conviction of an appearance are palpable and the critical expectation that we deny such convictions on the grounds that the image is unreal, or collusive, or demagogic, seems to imply that we are willing to deny ourselves something about our own experiential lives.

The *Ten Theses for an Aesthetics of Politics* thus posits the relation of aesthetics and politics as unsettled and, worse, uncritical. That is, these *Ten Theses* consider the possibility of a pre-judgmental moment of experience where our most heartfelt critical intuitions about how worlds ought to be ordered become undone. Crucial to this thought experiment is the advenience of an appearance that generates our senses of aesthetic appreciation and engenders a becoming–undoing of critical criteria. Needless to say, the *Ten Theses for an Aesthetics of Politics* take their inspiration from Jacques Rancière's own *Ten Theses on Politics* published in the virtual pages of *Theory and Event* as well as from Rancière's work on aesthetics and politics in general. Other sources of inspiration include Hannah Arendt's invocation of a politics of appearances, Stanley Cavell's writings on film and aesthetic experience, Roland Barthes's writings on photography that source the term "advenience" I pillage, as well as Michael Fried, Jean-Luc Nancy, and a host of other cited and uncited tongues. In short my loyalties will seem obvious to the reader, as will the various orthodoxies to which I'm responding. For further clarifications and elaborations, I have published essays and blog posts that elaborate on the abstractions in these pages. If the reader is interested, they may peruse those pieces listed under the "Further Writings" section at the end of this book.

One final note: I wish to express much gratitude to all those who shared their time and indulged my ruminations.

Thesis 1. On Advenience

An advenience is the ingression of an appearance. An appearance is the luminous partiality that strikes one's sensorium. The advenience of an appearance is thus the bodying forth of a luminosity that affronts our regard. As an effrontery, as an intensity of interface, the advenience of an appearance is an event of resistance.

BY "ADVENIENCE" I REFER to the capacity of things to stand forth or affront the spectator and, through this bodying forth, to strike at one's perceptual milieu. An advenience is the projecting outward of an appearance: a sound, a sight, a touch that, though perhaps always available, becomes obstinately perspicuous at the moment of its bodying forth. The challenge—both aesthetic and political—is to come to terms with this perspicuity. That an appearance advenes because of an intensity of projection means that we cannot rely on preexisting norms or criteria for making sense of the appearance. Indeed, the making sense of an appearance is precisely what the advenience denies. To regard an advenience is to allow the possibility of an absorptive be/holding ("Thesis 2: On Be/holding") that disarticulates our subjectivities from the structures of interest that conduct our habits of sense making. The advenience of an appearance interrupts the linear necessity of cause and effect.

An advenience is not an epistemic object: it has neither attributes, nor qualities, and there is nothing substantive about it. To handle an advenience as an object of epistemic interest, or even as a representational object whose nature it is to index something in the world, is to deny it its emergent luminosity and, thus, to deny it its singularity and its friction. It is, moreover, an attempt to affirm that adveniences belong to us, that they are for us. This is the conceit of the hermeneutic pursuit of meaning. To designate an advenience exclusively as an epistemic object (i.e., as a substance that appeals principally to our cognitive, meaning-making faculties) presumes a compellant must that affirms sense making as a validity criteria. This is the necessity of interest espoused by an epistemic mode of handling adveniences.

But to affirm the interest of an advenience is to concede that the function of appearances is to represent. Our narratocratic impulses are such that we treat appearances as referential substances.[1] "This painting represents a house" or "that image reifies our subjectivity." But before an object engages our cognitive capacities, it interfaces with our sensorialities. In short, before an appearance may be said to refer, it advenes; and at the level of its advenience, the appearance does not afford instructions for designating its own reference.

The advenience of an appearance exists prior to the "this" or the "that" of political judgment. Paradoxically, an advenience is the *a priori* that denies *a prioris* their power of privilege. When an appearance advenes, it does so in such a way that it cannot be

1. Davide Panagia, *The Political Life of Sensation* (Durham, N.C.: Duke University Press, 2010), 11–16.

either classified or categorized according to established criteria. The advenience of an appearance thus emerges in the interstice between sensation and reference. This is its political ontology. An advenience has an intangible punctuality about it. It touches us with a hapticity that cannot be reciprocated; and its touch is at once undetermined and unexpected ("Thesis 6: On the *Noli me tangere*"). Indeed, we can say that it is precisely the intangible hapticity of an advenience that disturbs our indexical prurience, our desire to scratch the itch of referentiality.

Consider a photograph. Roland Barthes says this: "I should like to know what there is in it that sets me off. So it seemed that the best word to designate (temporarily) the attraction certain photographs extend upon me was *advenience* or even *adventure*. This picture *advenes*, that one doesn't."[2] The term "advenience" has a brief half-life in Barthes's text as it is quickly replaced by his famous *punctum*, about which he has much to say and about which much has been written. But whereas the *punctum* emphasizes the strikingness of an appearance (it is, after all, a wound that pricks or bruises us; that is, a violence that dislocates our subjectivity), an advenience regards the pure fact of appearance, regardless of its effects. For something to advene means that it is an incomplete becoming, or an emergence that strikes without designating. An advenience is at once wholly present and always partial—one might wish to call it a perspicuous no-part (see "Thesis 4: On Aspectuality").

It should be of no surprise, then, that Barthes's little volume on photography is as obsessed as it is with hapticity: the hapticity of handling and the hapticity of looking. The photograph handles us by touching us, and we handle it by wanting

2. Roland Barthes, *Camera Lucida: Reflections on Photography*, trans. Richard Howard (New York: Hill and Wang, 1981), 19.

to put our finger on the detail of its *punctum*. The insufficiency of indexicality is also why Barthes affirms that he will not be guided by the consciousness of his thoughts when engaging adveniences, though he is "determined to be guided by the consciousness of my feelings."[3] Barthes is, of course, well aware that such exercises are fraught with failure. The willfulness of our minds is powerless at the interface with an advenience. We cannot touch the advening appearance in the manner in which it touches us. We are tempted to do so—in fact, this is our most basic instinct. We want to confirm the shareability of a "there it is, do you sense it, too?" This desire to confirm the presence of an intangible aspect is also why, in another important moment of Barthes's little book, he affirms that "I have always wanted to remonstrate with my moods; not to justify them."[4]

To remonstrate with one's moods suggests an order of handling not available to epistemic indexicality. We will never know what there is in the advenience that strikes us. And that is because there is no criteria or norm that determines what is striking in any appearance. Paradoxically, then, an advenience *does* indicate: but it does not refer. The advenience of an appearance is an emergent source of dislocation that neither commands nor determines a mode of attention. Simply put, I cannot remonstrate the allure of an appearance with any accuracy; this is despite the fact that my conviction of the appearance's singularity is absolute and unflappable. Hence the nonnecessity of having to justify one's moods.

This is what aesthetic disinterest ultimately means: the absence of a structure of interest that would guarantee a necessary causal relation between an advenience and a referent,

3. Ibid., 10.
4. Ibid., 18.

between a cause and an effect. To be clear, disinterest does not correspond to the positivist aspiration of value neutrality. On the contrary, disinterest refers to a temporal interval that suspends the binds of interest and initiates a state of abeyance when peoples, things, and other entities are no longer subject to conventional criteria of appraisal. Disinterest is, in this regard, the disarticulation of the constancies of correspondence that would or could afford value a representational structure. It is a pre-judgmental interstice.

The advenience of an appearance is thus an intensity of resistance to the *a priori* of interest—cognitive, political, economic, or otherwise. Whereas an armature of interest is such that it assigns a privilege to the knowing of things, the advenience of an appearance resists the privileges of the proper affirmed by practices of assignation and designation. Thinking of Cayce Pollard's (from William Gibson's *Pattern Recognition*) curious allergy to corporate logos, we might make our point this way: an object becomes a commodity (i.e., instrumental and useable) if—and only if—it exists within a structure of interest. The moment when that structure is lanced, the commodity status of the object is dislocated. By grinding away the logos on her jeans and other CPUs (Cayce Pollard Units), Cayce wants to "disinterest" objects.

Such considerations help explain why an aesthetics of politics cannot rely exclusively on the cognitivist critique of ideological stultification. The theory of stultification always already determines the structure of interest that conducts the arrival of an advenience (i.e., as an epistemic object), as well as the subjectivity of spectatorship (i.e., the knowing or duped subject) and its power of interest (i.e., domination). For the theory of stultification, all objects are necessarily commodities, and all sensing is fetishism. But politics is not exclusively the subjugation of power on the powerless, and aesthetics is not reducible to the truth/falsity distinction that the episteme of stultification sustains. To put this slightly differently, an advenience is not an object of cognitive interest; indeed, it has no-part in interest. As such, we cannot possess an advenience, nor does it capture us. The best that is available is an absorptive be/holding.

Thesis 2. On Be/holding

Be/holding is the bearing of the burden of resistance that the advenience of an appearance introduces. To be/hold does not suggest a passive viewership: it designates an active participation in the curatorial handling of an appearance's ingression. To be/hold is to look, but it is also a holding up to view, or a handling as a view, of that which bodies forth: it is to look but also to hold an appearance in regard. Be/holding thus regards an absorptive attention to the world that is a basic concern for an aesthetics of politics.

WE ARE ACCUSTOMED to those disenchantments that associate the terms "beholding," "absorption," and "spectatorship" with a condition of subjugation imposed by societies of the spectacle. The spectator is subjugated to a kind of imagistic power akin to a burning bush whose influence illumines and designates a moral code. In many accounts of the aesthetics of politics that desire to expose the lie of the image, the structure and shape of spectatorship remains at the level of propagandistic indoctrination so that all appearances operate like a Madison Avenue advertisement; as if, once again, all appearances exist and work within a unitary and universal structure of interest.

This mode of handling the image was first discovered by the Byzantine iconoclasts who disseminated a fear of the image's collusive effects.[1] Today, such handlings are also carriers of an inegalitarian pedagogy, rigidly partitioned between those who can know (i.e., the critic) and those who cannot know (i.e., the audience) the truth of the image.

But as Machiavelli advised long ago, political actors have always been handlers of appearances, partaking in an appearance's advenience. The advenience of the appearance thus resists this iconoclastic line of disenchantment. It is no doubt true that we live in a time besieged by appearances; it is equally true that we always have lived in such times. The proliferation of appearances, like the proliferation of words, is a feature of political life in general; and the alarmist response that wants to halt the flow of images and words, as well as the improper intermingling of words with images, is as prolific and enduring as the practices of image circulation themselves.

In contrast, the diacritical slash we insert in the word be/ holding wants to signal a pluralized sense of spectatorship as at once a "regarding," a "bearing," and a "tending to." Here we are reminded of Robert Warshow's ruminations (writing in 1954) on going to the movies: "I go to the movies for the same reason that the 'others' go: because I am attracted to Humphrey Bogart or Shelley Winters or Greta Garbo; because I require the absorbing immediacy of the screen; because in some way I take all that nonsense seriously."[2]

1. Marie-José Mondzain, *Image, Icon, Economy: The Byzantine Origins of the Contemporary Imaginary*, trans. Rico Franses (Stanford, Calif.: Stanford University Press, 2005).

2. Robert Warshow, *The Immediate Experience: Movies, Comics, Theatre, and Other Aspects of Popular Culture* (Cambridge, Mass.: Harvard University Press, 1962), xlii.

A be/holding is a curatorial mood that tends to the ways in which the multitudinous practices endured for bearing the frictions of an advenience are taken seriously (see "Thesis 7: On Interface"). It is not merely a looking, then, but a holding up to view, or the supporting of a view—as a frame supports the canvas or a screen supports a film projection. It is basic to the idea of democratic citizenship that individuals are said to have views. But this is a misnomer; a view is not something you have, it is something you bear for others to be/hold.

Hence the structure of interface that emerges with the advenience of an appearance: As we have already suggested, an advenience is an intangibility unavailable to our indexical impulses. We might conclude that we cannot hold an advenience; and yet we be/hold it, we attend to it. We bear the burden of a prurience that an advenience provokes: the prurience of at once wanting to make our sense of conviction of the appearance explicit, *and* not having at our disposal a shared structure of interest (or a consensus) that we might access as the source for confirming a shared appeal. In short, our be/holding an advenience is not the same as possessing an insight about its truth or meaning.

Be/holding does not mark a possession but rather an intangible hapticity, a dispossession. There is no concrete validity here because neither the be/holder, nor the maker, nor the object holds the power to dictate a mode of subjectivity appropriate to an advenience. Indeed, it cannot, because the instant of advenience is not determined by any necessary cause or relation. To be absorbed by the advenience of an appearance is thus precisely *not* to be "taken in" (or duped) by the image. Rather, the experience of an absorptive be/holding affords an interval in subjectivity that emerges at the instant of advenience. An advenience thus does not presuppose a voyeur; rather, it commends acts of regard, or practices of handling (see "Thesis 5: On Handling"). An aesthetics of politics thus takes aesthetic experience as relevant to political life because our microcultural practices of interface with aesthetic objects source our "practices of governance" of one another.[3] To the extent that we are all advening appearances to one another, the manners, attitudes, and forms of handling we enlist to be/hold appearances is of central concern to our understandings of the forces of collectivity that make a political handling-with-others at once thinkable and possible.

As advening appearances to one another, we are all partial luminosities. This means that the be/holder is not directed by any specific form of subjectivity, nor determined by any one picture of humanness. Be/holding is not a subject position assigned by the appearance forcing itself on me, and advenience is not a force of imposition. But it is an effrontery. Indeed, the dislocation of subjectivity ushered by an advenience makes any figuration of the subject impossible. We cannot know in advance the shape, disposition, or nature of a be/holder because the principle of nonnecessity that structures the emergence of an advenience denies us the capacity of predicting what human subjectivity will be like. Objects can be be/holders as much as people can; and people can be adveniences as much as objects can. There is a fundamental indistinction here between human and nonhuman.[4] Simply put, the be/holder is not human, but a human

3. James Tully, *Public Philosophy in a New Key: Volume 1, Democracy and Civic Freedom* (Cambridge, U.K.: Cambridge University Press, 2008), 21. Here Tully states that "one might take as a provisional field of inquiry 'practices of governance,' that is, the forms of reason and organization through which individuals and groups coordinate their various activities and the practices of freedom by which they act within these systems, either following the rules of the game or striving to modify them."

4. The indistinction between human and nonhuman has been amply documented by such diverse thinkers as Donna Haraway, Gilles

something; and as a something, the be/holder has no privileged stance, or stake, or access to the advenience. The be/holder is not he or she that knows the advenience and thus can speak its truth. Rather, the be/holder is an indeterminate emergence that arises at the interval of the advenience's ingression. We might say this: the be/holder and the advenience are becomings emergent from the event of interface.

The punctuality of an advenience procures a suspension of subjectivity whose resistance we handle through our practices of be/holding. Rather than being a disenchanted term of collusion, therefore, be/holding regards an indeterminate posture of attention one holds vis-à-vis a world that advenes. To be concerned with be/holding is thus to invite a curatorial mood into our political reflections by giving emphasis to the capacity for an active spectatorship that views and handles a point of view, that interfaces with it, bears it, and brings it into view—or projects it—for others to be/hold. The experience of be/holding discomposes our sensibilities and compels a reconfiguration of our affinities—not only with ourselves and the world, but also between ourselves and others. The diverse practices of be/holding are thus a central site of reflection for an aesthetics of politics.

Deleuze, and Stanley Cavell. In each instant, the case is made (in divergent ways) that the difference between human and nonhuman is tenable only if there are uncontested criteria for humanness. Thus the cyborg, or the BwO, or the automaton only counts as nonhuman from the perspective of a discourse that sustains the organic organization of humanness. But as Cavell's "striptease of misery" illustrates (*The Claim of Reason* [New York: Oxford University Press, 1999], 403–11), the perfected automaton poses the question of whether there can be care for a human something. Whatever answer we may give requires that we take very seriously the idea—first advanced by Hume in his elaboration of a discontinuous self, and then by cinema in its projection of actors on a screen—that we are all simply human somethings.

Thesis 3. On Immediacy

Immediacy is the temporality of an aesthetics of politics. When an appearance advenes, it strikes an impression on a sensorial apparatus, variously conceived. In doing so, it disarticulates our senses of constancy, continuity, and commonality. The immediacy of an aesthetics of politics is thus rooted in an ontology of discontinuity.

THE INGRESSION OF AN APPEARANCE OCCURS IN an instant, which is why it cannot be predicted, nor can it be anticipated or arranged. Consider the manner in which one is struck by a particularly compelling detail—of a song, of a movie, or of a swash of color on a painting. However overpowering—or not—the experience may be, it nonetheless is of the moment. It occurs instantaneously and one generates a sense of conviction regarding the vitality of the thing experienced, as if the thing were real and wholly present. This is the prestige, the conjuror's reveal, of the aesthetic object: it affords an immediate sensation of concreteness that resists the necessity of having to validate its actuality.

This temporality has worried many critics of the aestheticization of politics thesis. That is, the immediacy of aesthetic experience makes any appeal to aesthetics seem at once irrational and politically terrifying. But to say this amounts to a rejection tout court of the role of sensation in political life. Nothing about sensation is cognitive or cogent, though this does not mean that one does not reflect on one's sensations. These two conclusions do not follow. Rather, what does follow is that the temporality of immediacy that comes with an experience of sensation is of a different order of becoming than the terrapin pace of judgment. What the aestheticization of politics thesis takes for granted, therefore, is that politics is a cognitive activity resulting from ratiocination, and that political action must be calculated and considered. The alternative is unacceptable because anything that is not reasoned is politically dangerous.

But this conclusion seems rash. It carries with it the exclusivity of a substance ontology that imagines that the only things that exist in the world are, in fact, static substances, that there are no processes, and that politics is a realm of predictable behavior. However, the variability introduced by an ontology of immediacy exposes this fallacy of misplaced consistency by making apparent that even something as seemingly still and crystalline as a political concept is a wave of variable amplitude. As Michel de Montaigne once remarked in his essay "Of Repentance," "Even constancy itself is no other but a slower and more languishing motion."[1]

To appreciate the fullness of this point, consider for a moment what occurs at the instant of impression: on the surface of any body, an impression strikes and leaves a mark. But that mark inevitably fades, like the letters impressed on printed manuscripts, or a bruise on the skin, or the patina of celluloid, or the tread of a tire, or the scuff on a floor, or a publication in an

1. Michel de Montaigne, *The Complete Essays of Montaigne*, trans. Donald M. Frame (Stanford, Calif.: Stanford University Press, 1976), 611.

academic journal. The punctuality of an impression is variable, and its weight lightens in time, as does one's memory of it.

David Hume's insistence on the immediacy of impressions gives full expression to an ontology of discontinuity for an aesthetics of politics, as when he advises in his *Treatise of Human Nature* that when one begins "with the SENSES, 'tis evident these faculties are incapable of giving rise to the notion of *continu'd* existence of their objects, after they no longer appear to the senses."[2] There is a fragile relation between the advenience of an appearance, an impression, and continuity that for Hume is dissipated at the instant when the partiality of the appearance departs. This, in the end, is also the basis for his conception of civil society that is rooted in the idea of reputation as that variable impression that individuals impress on one another. Indeed, for Hume, civil society is a fragile and discontinuous advenience. Hence the importance of such customary practices as promising, which Hume compares to the Catholic doctrine of transubstantiation and holy orders. Promises are those alchemical artifices we devise to grant temporary constancy to an otherwise inconstant world.

Furthermore, Hume's ideas on impressions, their vivacity, and their punctuality suggests that there is no overarching impression, force, or criterion that will govern which aspects must stand forth as more relevant than others. Impressions can arise from anywhere or anything. Because their occurrence is immediate, impressions do not possess privilege. I take this to be the central aesthetic insight that Hume's ontology makes available. That is, according to Hume, we have no overarching rule or criterion that will determine which impression will count more than others,

2. David Hume, *A Treatise of Human Nature*, ed. David Fate Norton and Mary J. Norton (New York: Oxford University Press, 2000), 1.4.2.3, p. 126.

which will rule our ways of being, acting, and thinking, and which will dictate how one ought to compose one's existence. Because an impression is immediate and because immediacy denies constancy or predictability, then we cannot presume that our world is exclusively a world of substances. Rather, for Hume, the world is besieged by processes.

Such a process ontology extends to a discontinuity of self, which is the ultimate challenge of Hume's radical empiricism. For him, the self is an interim that fluctuates between states of becoming. To the extent that we can ever only know ourselves through our senses—because our sense of self is only ever an impression of self—then our selves are discontinuous partialities, immediate impressions that alter, fade, and terminate. The nature of an impression's discontinuity is thus contingent because there is no necessary relation between its effect and a preexisting cause; to put this slightly differently, there is no law of causality in the mere fact of series.[3] The determination of cause and effect are, for Hume, always retroactive; they are principles of association that contract the discontinuity between punctual impressions.

Immediacy is thus a marker of finitude. This fact also helps explain the disciplinary resistance to an aesthetics of politics in political theory and political science.[4] Finitude is unpredictable and variable: we can never know when we will die, we only know that we will die. The pressure of finitude is so heavy that we devise a variety of speculative metaphysics that assuage the anxiety of finitude's discontinuity so as to assure us that the immediacy of life itself might possess infinite constancy. It is not the intention here to endorse or deny the truth of such spec-

3. Robert Nozick, *Invariances: The Structure of the Objective World* (Cambridge, Mass.: Harvard University Press, 2001), 126–28.

4. Anne Norton, *95 Theses on Politics, Culture, and Method* (New Haven, Conn.: Yale University Press, 2004). See especially theses 67–69.

ulations, but only to affirm that their availability and political import are a confirmation of the ontology of discontinuity that imbues political life. By occupying the temporality of immediacy, an aesthetics of politics makes an ontology of discontinuity central to one's political considerations.

Thesis 4. On Aspectuality

An aspect is a no-part: it is a durational intensity that bodies forth contours of proximity that potentiate processes of intonation between advening appearances. The partaking of aspectuality is juxtapositive, where distinct entities bestow mutual inflection one on the other. An aspectual interface is thus something we grasp, not something we know.

WHAT ARE THE FORCES of relations between things? How do objects relate to be/holding and to one another? An aesthetics of politics makes available the fact that all adveniences are partialities whose relational mode is neither causal nor comparative, but aspectual. Thus, an aspectual affinity informed, as it is, by emergent incipiences of advenience, commends neither lineal nor arboreal causality, neither contrast nor resemblance, but juxtaposition. More to the point, what we discover when we explore an aspectual mood of engagement with the world is the extent to which juxtaposition imbues all relations such that we begin to conceive relations in terms of "this and that" rather than "this or that."

The temporality of immediacy and the ontology of discontinuity that arise in an aesthetics of politics emphasize the partiality of things. Phenomenologists have always insisted on the limits of our perception by suggesting that we ever only approach objects partially, and that their wholeness is unavailable to us.[1] This is a point that, as we have seen, had also been raised by David Hume when he advanced the idea that to experience something with our senses is necessarily to experience that thing as a partiality, or what he calls a "broken appearance."[2]

This is distinctly different from saying that one always has a partial perspective of the world. In other words, we are not here defending a version of perspectivilism that always assumes: (1) that objects are complete and unitary despite our partial perceptions; (2) that our mode of attention is cognitive to the extent that we can always surmise the difference between a part and a whole; and (3) that our perceptions distort our realities. To say that an advenience is a perspicuous no-part is to affirm the partiality of all things and thus resist the urge to completion or fulfillment of what is lacking: all that we have—all that we are—is parts.

It is Jacques Rancière who more than any other contemporary thinker has advanced a vertiginous defense of the participatory nature of partialities. His thesis, that all politics involves first and foremost a "partition of the sensible," emphasizes the relational dimensions of things: a partition is simultaneously an interruption and a sharing, it is at once an attachment and a detachment, a cutting up and distribution of lots. But a "partition" also shares an etymology with the Latin *parere*, meaning to appear: an appearance is in this sense a part, an aspect. A partition of the sensible thus refers to the armatures of artifice that render appearances sensate. The political dimension of

---

1. Maurice Merleau-Ponty, *Phenomenology of Perception*, trans. Colin Smith (New York: Routledge, 2002), 182.
2. Hume, *Treatise of Human Nature*, 1.4.2.36, p. 136.

aesthetics is precisely not to uncover the apparent partiality of things, or to expose the falsity of partial truths, but to ascertain and render palpable how structures of feeling make appearances count. The part of those who have no-part, we might conclude, is Rancière's political ontology of the *punctum* that finds relevance in the practices of partaking of and in appearances. For Rancière, to appear and to partake are synonyms of one another and of democratic politics in general.

To the extent that an aspect is a no-part, it is the improper element that strikes in an entirely unpredictable manner and that interrupts circulation through its advenience (see "Thesis 9: On Impropriety"). It is an event of resistance. This is the reason why we affirmed the fact of be/holding in the face of an advenience, and the intoning of inflection as an aspect's partition of the sensible. The friction of an advenience's interface resists the expectation of signification or meaning, it resists tropological understanding. Aspects are impressions that emerge in the immediacy of an advenience. As impressions, they are necessarily partial and discontinuous in exactly the manner in which Hume recommends. We cannot know an aspect; the best that we can do is grasp it's juxtapositive impropriety.[3]

Ludwig Wittgenstein's considerations on acts of naming and other related practices in his *Philosophical Investigations* are as relevant to our thesis as are Rancière's disquisitions on partitions of the sensible: one might say that Rancière and Wittgenstein intone aspects of one another. Consider section 38 of the *Philosophical Investigations*: "Naming appears as a

3. On grasping as a mode of understanding in political theory, see the first volume of James Tully's *Public Philosophy in a New Key*, 66. On aspect change as a democratic practice, see Aletta Norval's *Aversive Democracy* (Cambridge, U.K.: Cambridge University Press, 2007), esp. 126–40.

queer connexion of a word with an object.—And you really get such a queer connexion when the philosopher tries to bring out *the* relation between name and thing by staring at an object in front of him and repeating a name or even the word 'this' innumerable times. For philosophical problems arise when language *goes on holiday*. And *here* we may indeed fancy naming to be some remarkable act of mind, as it were a baptism of an object."[4] Philosophers like Saul Kripke and cultural theorists like Slavoj Žižek have characterized this famous passage in Wittgenstein's writings as expressing a commitment to something like branding—that is, the fixing of a name to a thing through time. Juxtaposing ourselves to this explanation, we might add a rejoinder and say that this passage *projects* the complexities of naming that it displays. Here—and throughout the *Philosophical Investigations* more generally—Wittgenstein is not involved in exposing an argument about naming; he is, rather, bearing a picture of the ways in which we be/hold the advenience of appearances and the handlings we develop (i.e., naming) to tend to our be/holdings. And this is what Wittgenstein means when he says that "naming appears as a *queer* connexion of a word with an object." It appears as a queer connexion because what naming does is generate intermediary aspects that intone modes of proximity between objects—like the lines of a drawing of a duck/rabbit that at once suggest superimposition and juxtaposition. The practice of naming is a queer way of laying witness to our absorption with an apparent world.

Wittgenstein expands on this insight in another passage from the *Philosophical Investigations*:

4. Ludwig Wittgenstein, *Philosophical Investigations: The English Text of the Third Edition*, trans. G. E. M. Anscombe (New York: Macmillan, 1973), §122.

A main source of our failure to understand is that we do not *command a clear view* of the use of our words.—Our grammar is lacking in this sort of perspicuity. A perspicuous representation produces just that understanding which consists in "seeing connexions." Hence the importance of finding and inventing *intermediate cases.*

  The concept of a perspicuous representation is of fundamental significance for us. It earmarks the form of account we give, the way we look at things. (Is this a "Weltanschauung"?)[5]

Once again, the problem of "seeing connexions" is central to our experiences of an apparent world. Our ways of handling adveniences, including our pictures of a language, compel us to develop affinities between ourselves and a world that appears, and these affinities are what give perspicuity to the world. That is, the capacity to artifice *"queer* connexions" represents a curatorial mood for attending to the world, a practice by which we admit the ingression of things and through which we express our own absorption with the appearances that circulate about us. Finally, the perspicuous representations that arise from our practices of queering connections are projections that we give to the appearance of things; it is our mode of touching and handling without ever penetrating or exposing. Such connexions are thus queer precisely because a willingness to connect with what appears is stifled by an advenience's resistance to acts of definition or designation.

  In short, Wittgenstein's appeal to queerness allows us to query the account of comprehension through communication in theories of consensus-oriented political deliberation. There is no comprehension between groups, identities, or works; at best, there may be a queer connexion between them, or an aspectual affinity that intones proximities. But such intonations

5. Ibid.

are the generative emergence of a be/holding. For a pluralist politics to demand comprehension or understanding is thus to deny the partiality of things, and to impose a substance ontology on partialities. It is to insist that coherence, communication, and consensus are the only possible political goals, that antagonism is always dialectic, and that the movement of history is teleological. To make a fetish of agreement in this way is to turn a blind eye to a politics of resistance.

Rather than consensus, resemblance, and comprehension, an aesthetics of politics proposes an aspectual interface of emergent adveniences. The grasping of an aspect thus regards an absorptive partaking of and with the intonations of proximity that emerge from the juxtaposition of adveniences. Aspectuality is the mode of relating for an aesthetics of politics.

Thesis 5. On Handling

We be/hold an advenience by handling it. But to handle something is not the same as using it. The handling proposed by an aesthetics of politics regards microcultural practices of arrangement and disposition. In this respect, an aesthetics of politics proposes that our handling of the advenience of an appearance projects our handling of one another. Another term we might use to indicate our handling of one another is practices of governance.

OUR ENGAGEMENT WITH THE WORLD of appearances involves a handling that regards the abilities of peoples, things, and events to interact and interface with those aspectual somethings that strike. The world is replete with practices of handling: the leaf handles the parasite, the concierge handles the package, the wind handles the spore, the painter handles the brush, the factory worker handles the minimum wage, the algorithm handles the data, the camera handles the film, the beholder handles the appearance, *and* (most importantly) *vice versa*: the brush handles the painter like the keyboard handles the writer; the film handles the camera like the ink handles the pen; the spore handles the wind like the string handles the guitar. Handling is a microcultural practice that expresses the persistence of incipient trajectories of awareness and immersion. A central contention of an aesthetics of politics, therefore, regards the handling of adveniences and how such handlings mutually inflect our handling of one another. Rather than an epistemological handling that commands an argumentative dogmatism vis-à-vis one's political engagements with others, an aesthetics of politics commends a curatorial regard for our handlings of the adveniences of appearances.

Our practices of handling make explicit the political question of certainty: what is it that we want to remonstrate when we be/hold an advenience? But to be fair to our microcultural practices of handling, we must resist the epistemic urge to associate one's interface with objects with the specification of an object's identity or function. An act of handling is less a skill or a techne than an occurrence. A handling arises from what the philosopher Martin Heidegger refers to as our "concernful dealings" with the world and those things, peoples, and events that populate it.[1] Thus a dealing, or a handling (both these words are translations of Heidegger's *Umgang*) is not a cognitive activity, though this does not mean it is unreflective either. Rather, a handling regards our abilities to engage objects beyond our interest in them. Heidegger's insistence on handling wants to resist the urge to reduce one's dispositions to the world in terms of interest. One does not handle something because one is interested in it, or because it is useful. The microcultural practices of handling that speak to our curatorial attentions to the world regard that which moves in and through one's be/holdings.

Let's invoke an example from an activity most of us partake in when reading: that of highlighting, or underlining—that is,

1. Martin Heidegger, *Being and Time*, trans. John Macquarrie and Edward Robinson (New York: HarperPerennial, 2008), 102.

the practice and act of indexing—what we sense as relevant in a work. What is it that compels us to underline the passage we do underline when we underline a passage in a book? What is it about that sentence, or phrase, or utterance that we wish to emphasize when underscoring a notable passage? The rendering remarkable through highlighting is a handling. When marking a passage we remark to ourselves (or others) "pay attention to this; be impressed by it, as I have been impressed." By marking our absorptions, we render the passage remarkable. The highlighted passage becomes something that stands out, an appearance that advenes and impresses on our curatorial attentions.

We can give many interested answers as to why the passage does stand out, or ought to. It may be the thesis of an essay, or a particularly useful formulation of a problem, or the infamous "what's at stake" conclusion of an argument. But all these explanations merely suggest that we bear a capacity for remarking that allows us to exact a passage of note. And to say this is merely to say that our curatorial dispositions render us appraisers. Any other reader can and might underline any other passage for any other reason; the content of the passage does not count as evidence for one's emphasis because that content may change whenever we read a work anew. And if you want an example, just go back to a book you've read more than once and see if the passages you underlined then are the same as the ones you underlined a few years later, or would underline today.

What this suggests is that the sole source of purpose for work is not its informational value: it is not the bearer of intention (whether authorial or otherwise). There is nothing in the text that tells me that I must highlight this passage here, or that part of the text there, or the passage on the next page. A passage strikes me and I highlight it for a million reasons; but the work itself does not instruct on the value and site of its own interest. The inconstancy of the work is such that it is not interested in accounting for its use. Hence the force behind Heidegger's own insistence that "no matter how sharply we just *look* [Nur-noch-hinsehen] at the 'outward appearance' ["Aussehen"] of Things in whatever form it takes, we cannot discover anything ready-to-hand. If we look at Things just 'theoretically,' we cannot get along without understanding ready-to-hand. But when we deal with them by using them and manipulating them, this activity is not a blind one; it has its own kind of sight, by which our manipulation is guided and from which it acquires its specific Thingly character."[2] In other words, handling invokes a be/holding that is not myopic in its orientation toward interest or use.

Rather, the kind of attention we are calling be/holding arises at the moment when the interest of an object is disrupted or interrupted, like Heidegger's famous broken hammer. The terms he uses to refer to this disruption are "conspicuousness," "obtrusiveness," and "obstinacy." Each of these terms refers to an interruption in one's relation to an object, where one feels helpless toward the object because it is somehow out of joint and no longer available in the manner to which one is accustomed. "The tool," he says, "turns out to be damaged or the material unusable."[3] We are absorbed by the object's broken handling, at which point an entire universe opens itself up to us. Handling exists within a universe of disinterest and our concernful awareness arises from the interface with disinterested things; this is because once disinterested, they are freed from purposiveness.

Think back to the highlighting example and how the underscored passage breaks the presupposed totality of the work; and now think of how anxious many of us feel about marking a book

2. Ibid., 98.
3. Ibid., 103.

for the first time, or about that first scuff on a brand new pair of shoes. We are anxious of disrupting its newness by marking it because once a part is underscored, the object no longer feels like a unity. There now are marks that parse it. We might put the matter this way: our concernful attention to the advenience of a passage that is remarkable in a piece of writing underscores the partiality of the work and makes available to our attentions aspects that would otherwise go unremarked if the work were a presupposed totality. As a part, the highlighted passage is a site of absorption: it just stands out and draws us in in such a way that any appeal to a specific interest in the work seems unreliable or, indeed, unnecessary. Or rather, our attention to that which stands out in a work is not justifiable in terms of necessity, causality, or function. That we may then make use of an underscored passage—for professional purposes, to give comfort to our woes, or to provide evidence for a developing argument—does not deny the fact that at the moment of its incipient advenience, it remains disinterested.

It is in this sense that we understand handling as active rather than passive, as a political activity of be/holding as well as a microcultural practice of interface that extracts us from the conventional logic of interest. The practices of handling we attend to in an aesthetics of politics procure an instance of disinterest that monstrously disfigures our conventions of attachment, as well as our habits of living (i.e., in the case of our example, we can no longer read the work in the same way after highlighting the text). At a very basic but fundamental level, the advenience of disinterest regards the ingression of a mode of monstrance that strikes at us and affords an attention to the appearance of things—not, that is, to explain them, but rather to concern ourselves with them. In this regard, a handling's disinterest bespeaks a curatorial absorption with the world.

Thesis 6. On the *Noli me tangere*

The handling of an advenience resists the kind of penetrative
touch that wants to expose the truth of an object. Rather than
expositive, an aesthetics of politics is in the mood of the noli me
tangere: *the "do not touch me" or "do not withhold me" of the*
appearance. The noli me tangere *regards an intangible hapticity*
that discomposes the expectations of possession.

LET US HANDLE SOME IMAGES. The figures below are famous
and taken from a biblical iconography of the story of Jesus. Their
theme is that of the hapticity of the image—specifically, the image of a deity—and they depict two instances of touching (or not
touching) the figure of Jesus in his role as the resurrected divinity.

Both works are remarkable.

In Caravaggio's *Doubting Thomas* (Figure 1), the doubting disci-
ple thrusts his hand into the side of Jesus in order to perforate his
existence and confirm his resurrected actuality. Thomas's touch at
once wants to expose and possess evidence of Jesus's resurrection.
Here the extended hand that handles the wound penetrates the
source of the sensation of belief so as to confirm that the image
of god is indeed present. Such confirmation promises to relieve
the pangs of doubt. Thomas's touch clutches the wound; it is an

Figure 1. Michelangelo Merisi da Caravaggio (1573–1610), *Doubting Thomas* (1601–1602). Oil on canvas, 107 × 146 cm. Inv. GK I 543. Stiftung Preussische Schlösser and Gärten Berlin-Brandenburg. Photo credit: bpk, Berlin (Bildergalerie, Potsdam / Gerhard Murza) / Art Resource, New York.

ostensive touch (like the one above described by Wittgenstein in his account of the philosopher's "this") that wants to point to the source of the sensation in order to hold on to one's faith. And notice, too, Caravaggio's subtleness in presenting us with two tears in the painting: Christ's wound and the seam of Thomas's torn garment (upper left shoulder). They are perpendicular to each other, they are painted along the same axis, and they are practically identical—and yet completely different. It's almost as if Caravaggio wants us to believe that one wound is real while the other is decorative—which would be completely in line with the thematics of the painting: here is the real image of god, Jesus Christ the mediator of truth and falsity. All you have to do is thrust your hand in the wound in order to look and see for yourself. Of course, the point of Caravaggio's painterly tear is not to prove the difference between a real and an ornamental wound, but to put on display the urge—and the temptation—of indexicality and verification. Thus, through Thomas's gesture of adhesion to a lesion, conviction is transformed into belief and a sensation is given a legitimating ground. Caravaggio's *Doubting Thomas*, in other words, dramatizes a desire to know the image, to touch it in such a way as to penetrate its externality and possess the source of its sensations so as to nail firmly in place the relation between sensation and reference.

The curious thing, of course, is that the event depicted in this painting has no biblical source. As Glenn Most has shown, there is no textual evidence of Thomas ever touching Jesus's wounds.[1] Thomas does doubt the existence of a raised body, but he does not touch the wound. Rather, imagining the touch as a hold is an artistic rendering of the prurience of iconographic hapticity: it does not represent the passage, but marks an aspect of the passage that regards the intense human desire to know and verify the impossible source of an advenience.

The second image we'll look at is Pontormo's *Noli me tangere* painting (Figure 2), which thematizes another order of hapticity that, we can say, lies closer to the practices of be/holding of an aesthetics of politics. This biblical scenario predates Jesus's encounter with the Doubting Thomas, but not by much. It refers to the moment when Jesus exits the tomb on the third day after his crucifixion and encounters Mary Magdalene who is in the garden, mourning his passing—a picture of the event of advenience if there ever was one. Astonished by his luminescence, Mary lunges towards Jesus in a dance-like embrace (as Pontormo pictures the gesture) while he sashays away from her, uttering the negative in-

1. Glenn W. Most, *Doubting Thomas* (Cambridge, Mass.: Harvard University Press, 2009).

Figure 2. Jacopo Pontormo (1494–1557), *Noli Me Tangere* (ca. 1532). Casa Buonarroti. Photo credit: Scala / Art Resource, New York.

junction *noli me tangere* (in Greek, *mê mou haptou*): "do not touch me," or "do not withhold me," or "do not hold me back." We might wish to paraphrase as follows: "be/hold me without possessing me," "hold me in your regard without clutching me." The interval of the *noli me tangere*, in other words, pictures the intangible hapticity that we lend an advenience, an ungraspable caress that attends to the appearance as it advenes. In this interval, there is a play of hapticity that never actually resolves but that nonetheless invites our ability to absorb and bear the scene. The be/holding that the advenience of appearance invites makes untenable the claim of possessive exposition: one cannot own an experience of advenience. On the contrary, the interval of advenience calls forth a curatorial regard of and for that which appears.

In his study of the relationship between sight and touch, spurred on by his looking at some *noli me tangere* paintings, Jean-Luc Nancy says this:

> What is seeing if not a deferred touch? But what is a deferred touch if not a touching that sharpens or concentrates without reserve, up to a necessary excess, the point, the tip, and the instant through which the touch detaches itself from what it touches, at the very moment when it touches? Without this detachment, without this recoil or retreat, the touch would no longer be what it is, and would no longer do what it does (or it would not let itself do what it lets itself do). It would begin to reify itself in a grip, in an adhesion or a sticking, indeed, in an agglutination that would grasp the touch in the thing and the thing within it, matching and appropriating the one to the other and then the one in the other. There would be identification, fixation, property, immobility. "Do not hold me back" amounts to saying "Touch me with a real touch, one that is restrained, nonappropriating and nonidentifying." Caress me, don't touch me.[2]

2. Jean-Luc Nancy, *Noli Me Tangere: On the Raising of the Body*, trans. Sarah Clift, Pascale-Anne Brault, and Michael Naas (New York: Fordham University Press, 2009), 49–50.

Nancy is talking about an experience of encounter that resists the possessive grasp of referentiality. He is, in short, talking about ownership and appropriation and how through the interval of advenience we encounter the possibility of there being a non-possessive hold—a be/holding. Alongside the history of liberalism's possessive individuals, we might conclude, there is a parallel and minoritarian history of aesthetic *dis*possession. Within this trajectory we learn that the advenience of an appearance resists the possessiveness of referentiality, and thus the kind of knowing that bespeaks epistemic ownership; but it also resists the possessiveness of the desire to hold, own, and use that which is ontologically intangible. What does it mean—we ask once again—to hold an appearance? An appearance cannot be held but can only be be/held. Thus concerns over possessive individualism are replaced by concerns over the organoleptic assignments and dispositional structures that are the matters of course for our attending to the disjunctures between person and world, between sensation and reference.

And is this not the problem of citizenship itself? Is citizenship not the advenience of a political subjectivity that has neither place, nor name, nor status, nor part; someone or something that cannot be held in its proper place? One of the crucial characteristics of the rise of the citizen–subject in the eighteenth century is the fact that it emerges out of a series of conditions of discontinuity: the citizen possesses neither title, nor rank, nor status. As such, it resists all systems of signification that require the holding of a name in order to count. That is, the *noli me tangere* of democratic citizenship resists the expectation of counting tout court. The citizen literally does not count—it does not refer to anything—because the citizen has no part. She is a partiality. Possession and reference, we might say, do not count in the face of the advenience of citizenship.

The crucial problem for an aesthetics of politics is thus the following: if the advenience of political subjectivities appear but do not count because an advenience is supernumerary to any criteria for counting, then what are the practices of handling and modes of attention we dispose to the *noli me tangere* of advenience?

Thesis 7. On Interface

Contemporary political life is characterized neither by the exchange of ideas, nor by the communication of intentions between speaking subjects. Rather, it is characterized by the microcultural dynamics of interface through and by which subjects and objects cast appearances. The iconomy of and interface with appearances is the principal feature of contemporary political life.

AS WE AFFIRMED in Thesis 6, possession is no longer the principal practice of holding in contemporary life. Few, if any of us, have possessions (despite our culture of consumerism). Even property has been shown to be virtually untethered to any ambition of possession, as the American subprime mortgage crisis demonstrated in the first decade of the new millennium. The shock effects of that cataclysm have been unfathomable, not only because they have ushered in a new age of wealth discrepancy and poverty, not only because they have decimated the ambitions and spirit of entire classes of peoples, but also because they have shaken to the core our inherited faith in political economy's linear causality of property, ownership, and status. To resist capitalism no longer means a resistance to property and structures of ownership: capitalism has already co-opted this strategy and made ownership irrelevant by making property ethereal. Instead, political resistance comes with the overthrowing of ownership as a privileged modality of holding.

Rather than holding, interface is now the dominant form of interaction: it is the posting, disseminating, and facing up to the iconomy of appearances. This is one of the many characteristics of politics in the age of cybernetics. Recall the emergence in 1984 of graphical user interface (GUI) technology popularized by Apple Computer's (then) new Macintosh. As Lev Manovich has described it, the rise of GUI and subsequent cut and paste technology (among many other software applications) resulted in a veritable gestalt switch in our modes of handling the intersect of cultural forms.[1] Simply consider the extent to which we now privilege screens—and especially touch screens—as our principal objects of handling.[2] From film, to TV, to the computer screen, to the cell phone screen, to the tablet, an inordinate amount of our time is spent interfacing with these mediators; we might half-jokingly call these our iconomic indicators.[3] Thus,

1. Lev Manovich, *The Language of New Media* (Cambridge, Mass.: MIT Press, 2001).

2. Anna McCarthy, *Ambient Television: Visual Culture and Public Space* (Durham, N.C.: Duke University Press, 2001).

3. We say "half-jokingly" because as Karin Knorr Cetina's ethnographies of investment culture have shown, the computer screen is—now—the principal site of what she calls "architectural flows" of investment/trader culture and financial markets: "Clearly, if the screen world is a flow-world then this has to do with the technologies, the dealing systems and the feeds of content that make up this world and account for its step-by-step change. Traders acting on screen contribute to the flow through the specific time span of their activities and the text they add, but the time span and the information requirements are pre-given by the screen world. Engrossment and responsiveness result from the narrow framing and temporal 'shortness' of the electronic lifeworld,

before we reflect on the sociality of Instagram, or Twitter, or the Internet on our political imaginaries and—indeed—on our political–economic practices (as the Twitter-inspired political movements have made urgent),[4] we must consider the practices of interface that emerge from an ontology of the screen.

Cinematicity is crucial to our iconophilia. Stanley Cavell is one of the first, and most insightful, thinkers to consider the screen and our interface with it as an important ontological condition of modern spectatorship, one that shares a history with the canvas and the photograph but is also notably different from both. In a short but incisive chapter titled "Photograph and Screen" of *The World Viewed*, he claims the following:

> The world of a moving picture is screened. The screen is not a support, not like a canvas; there is nothing to support, that way. It holds a projection, as light as light. A screen is a barrier. What does the silver screen screen? It screens me from the world it holds—that is, makes me invisible. And it screens that world from me. That the projected world does not exist (now) is its only difference from reality. (There is no feature, or set of features, in which it differs. Existence is not a predicate.) Because it is the field of a photograph, the screen has no frame; that is to say, no border. Its limits are not so much the edges of a given shape as they are the limitations, or capacity, of a container. The screen *is*

and from the existence of entrance conditions. We maintain that the network reality of earlier times where markets were not embodied on screen did not show this temporality and other features. We also believe that they resulted in similar engrossments only at certain moments, for example when markets were found and connected in arbitrage deals." Karin Knorr Cetina and Urs Bruegger, "Inhabiting Technology: The Global Lifeform of Financial Markets," *Current Sociology* 50, no. 3 (2002): 400–401.

4. Alex Nunns and Nadia Idle, *Tweets from Tahrir: Egypt's Revolution as It Unfolded, in the Words of the People Who Made It* (New York: OR Books, 2011).

a frame; the frame is the whole field of the screen—as a frame of
film is the whole field of a photograph, like the frame of the loom
or a house. In this sense, the screen-frame is a mold, or form.[5]

The screen bears a projection—it handles it by supporting its luminosity. This is one sense of how a movie pictures something
screened: it is light projected on a smooth surface. But a screen
is also a limit. In order to see the projected light, the be/holder
must be screened from the projection—one could say, here, that
the be/holder does not count to the projection, she is made invisible to it. The light does not shine on the spectator; rather, the
shining of the projected light on the screen obscures her. This
is a necessary condition for viewing a projected image. And it is
only through this projection onto the screen that the appearance
of the cinematic image can advene. That is, in order for the appearance to advene, we must be obscured; our *I* that is temporarily us—our subjectivity in light of this light, with all its expectations and desires to touch, to hold, or to grasp the appearance in
a knowing way—must be darkened, withdrawn, absorbed. This
is the significance of the screen's capacity to screen me from the
projected world, to render us invisible to it. The "I" is absorbed,
obscured—or, better yet, discomposed—when the projection is
projected. And this screening also screens that world from us.
The screen is thus a limit to our knowing and to our being able to
handle the world in a knowing manner—to our wanting to con-
tain the world by knowing it.

The screen *is* a mediator of interface. The political corollary
to this is that it is no longer the word, nor the pen, nor the piece
of paper, that may be said to count as the principal object of
political agency: the word *was* mightier than the sword, but

5. Stanley Cavell, *The World Viewed: Reflections on the Ontology of
Film* (Cambridge, Mass.: Harvard University Press, 1979), 24–25.

now the mouse is mightier than both sword and word. Though the modern political actor may have handled speaking and writing, the contemporary political actor no longer operates in a Gutenberg galaxy governed by the movements of word and deed. Her universe comprises microcultural practices of interface that screen appearances. The further corollary to this is that the materiality of political agency has also transubstantiated: the political actor is, like the actor on the screen, a human something, a partial appearance that advenes.

To engage the microcultural practices of interface that imbue our contemporary political culture requires our having to take seriously, in a manner heretofore unprecedented, the medium and media of interface, including the role of the media industry not simply as the site of a symbolic subjugation but as sources of access to networks of navigation. What enables interface and how is interface impeded—for instance—by the shutting down of Internet servers at the height of revolutionary tweeting?[6] Such questions require our having to rethink the ways in which our current modes of interchange extend beyond the exchange of words and ideas. The iconomic transmission of and interface with the advenience of an appearance is thus one of the central sites of attention for an aesthetics of politics.

6. One of the fascinating developments that emerged from practices of interface deployed during the 2011 revolution in Egypt is Hosni Mubarak's attempt to shut down Internet servers (on January 26, 2011) that lasted for five days. This did, indeed, interrupt the flow of tweets and Facebook posts. However, the one remaining Internet provider Mubarak did not shut down was the one used by Egypt's stock exchange, which quickly became a central hub for the transmission of illicit tweets. See Idle's introduction to Nunns and Idle, *Tweets from Tahrir*.

Thesis 8. On Luminosity

No object is political; no object is aesthetic. Objects are plurivalent permanences, luminous entities without cause or purpose. An aesthetics of politics thus does not refer to formulas for interpreting the political value of works of art; it addresses the modes in and through which the luminosity of an appearance is rendered available to perceptibility.

WE MIGHT SAY THAT OBJECTS (INCLUDING THOSE objects of analysis we call political subjectivities) have a life of their own, regardless of the intentional structures we deploy to make sense of them (see "Thesis 5: On Handling"). Our habits of political analysis operate in such a way as to establish the significance of things by integrating whatever object may seem relevant within a system of intentions that renders the object explicable and comprehensible. This is the great anthropomorphism of social science inquiry: that any object whatsoever—a state, a leader, an economy, an NGO, a party, an interest group, and so forth—has intentions and, as such, operates within a structure and akin to the human will. It is only in this way that we may then speak of an object's usefulness to our political reflections *and* to our political ambitions. As an *operandum* in a preconceived intentional structure, an object is thus said to be predictable and accountable (i.e., meaningful). It is also only in this way that we are enabled to justify the value of aesthetic objects to political thought: aesthetic objects are valuable—that is, have an interest and a purpose—because their intention appeals to a structure of belief that we either endorse or condemn.

But as we have said, the domain of an aesthetics of politics is one of disinterest and unpurposiveness: aesthetic experience is an event of discontinuity where no structure of interest or criteria of belief suffices to explain the value of an object—or, for that matter, the intentional structure *of* the experience. What this suggests is that the kind of explanatory system that makes intention, causality, and predictability necessary to signification is insufficient for an aesthetics of politics. This is why we say that no object is political, and no object is aesthetic. Our concern is not with the classification of a domain of interest that will explain the value of things. Any object whatever may be experienced aesthetico-politically—whether brush stroke, pop song hook, oil spill, policy initiative, kernel of information, sexual orientation, economic standing, weather pattern, word, image, and so forth.

The relevant category of experience is not the purposiveness of an object but the intensity of luminosity that strikes at our sense of conviction. But aesthetic conviction is a force of intensity available for experience, and not simply a quality in the human experience of things. It is not synonymous with perspectivilism; it is not the result of an interpretation from "my perspective." Aesthetic conviction arises at the interval of advenience and refers to the kind of luminous intensity that makes an object, or a detail, or a work, available for attention in a manner heretofore unremarked; this, despite the fact that the object in question may have always been apparent.

In this regard, and looking back to "Thesis 5: On Handling," we say that a brush handles the canvas as the painter handles the brush, or that a worker handles the minimum wage as the borrowing limit handles the debt crisis. But we can also say that the state is a handler, as is an NGO or a religion. And to say this is to suggest that the experience of which we speak is not exclusive to human interference. Rather, aesthetic conviction results from the immediacy of interface that arises from the interval of advenience. Conviction is unexplainable and unjustifiable; there is no necessity to its emergence.

An aesthetic of politics is responsive to a sensation of conviction, despite the fact that there is no source or site of evidence that will count as necessary or sufficient to that sensation. This is why the sense of absoluteness that accompanies aesthetic experience is not universalizable. This is also why we address the luminosity of adveniences rather than the political effectivity of works of art. The distinction we want to retain is between an object's luminosity and what it might illuminate. For an object to illuminate something, its shine must be indexical and directed at a referent: in this way, an object is imagined to operate like a spotlight that designates a marker on a stage. Illumination is entirely theatrical. An object's luminosity, however, disavows the directionality of the spotlight. A luminosity radiates without referencing: it forgoes the ostension of the spotlight as the principal mode of relation.

The distinction between illumination and luminosity thus suggests two divergent forms of political realism: the former (illumination) demands that a perspective be shareable and hence available for comprehension. This order of political realism (PR_1) requires the foundation of criteria for the identity of objects so that they may be said to refer to something real in the world. PR_1 is a referential realism that endorses a substance ontology: static entities with identifiable properties. A citizen has these rights; a political actor has these physical and psychological capabilities; politics involves states and governments, policies and interests—and each of these is a qualifiable substance that is verifiable as a concrete substance.

But there is a second order of political realism (PR_2) that is closer to the experience of aesthetic conviction spurred by luminosity. PR_2 does not address or explain substances because its realism is not indexical—there is nothing to illumine in PR_2, nothing to index. What kind of evidence could there be in order to verify the luminosity of an advenience? To say that an appearance advenes is thus not simply to define the properties of its motility, it is also to speculate on the processual forces that give it its ingressional properties. It is Alfred North Whitehead who first introduces the idea of ingression vis-à-vis objects in *The Concept of Nature*. For him, ingression refers to a mode of relation, and not simply the description of an action: it is the event of relation that arises from superimposition of objects whose contours remain unfinished. "The ingression of an object into an event," Whitehead affirms, "is the way the character of the event shapes itself in virtue of the being of the object. Namely the event is what it is, because the object is what it is."[1] Thus, object and event mutually inflect each other through a relational dynamic that sustains their fluid, rather than static, natures. In *Process and Reality* Whitehead calls this "a lure for feeling."[2]

The political realism (PR_2) proposed by an aesthetics of politics attends to the intensity of conviction that ingresses at the moment of advenience.

1. Alfred North Whitehead, *The Concept of Nature* (Seattle: CreateSpace Independent Publishing Platform, 2012), 144.
2. Alfred North Whitehead, *Process and Reality* (New York: Simon and Schuster, 2010), 25, 184–85.

Thesis 9. On Impropriety

Politics is improper. It is the interval of discontinuity that emerges from the immediacy of an advenience. What an aesthetics of politics thus makes available to political thinking is the fact that there has only ever truly been one rule for democracy: that there is no necessity of rule. This is why democratic politics is always already aesthetic.

THERE IS AN aspectual affinity between aesthetics and democracy: both sustain the nonnecessity of rule. Thus, both are improper. This does not mean that democracy is anarchic and without rules. It affirms that no rule is necessary to democracy.

In the political sense of the term, an impropriety is a wrong. But here we must not confuse the status of a wrong with the epistemological concept of a mistake. A wrong is not an error that needs correcting in order to return to the proper rule of things. It is not some flaw calling for reparation. As Jacques Rancière argues, "It is the introduction of an incommensurable at the heart of the distribution of speaking bodies."[1] What

1. Jacques Rancière, *Disagreement: Politics and Philosophy*, trans. Julie Rose (Minneapolis: University of Minnesota Press, 1999), 29.

might this mean, exactly? Simply put, the political wrong is the affirmation of an arresting conviction, or a site of resistance. When we affirmed that an advenience was "an event of resistance" ("Thesis 1: On Advenience"), we were affirming its status as an impropriety. An advenience is that which interrupts the organizations of perceptibility that make objects and values circulate properly.

Consider the example of Jackson Pollock's line in his works dating from the late 1940s, but especially *Number 1A, 1948*.[2] As is well-known, Pollock would pour paint onto a stretched canvas on the floor, creating massive tableaus with swirls of paint weaving throughout. As he famously affirmed in an interview, "My painting does not come from the easel. I hardly ever stretch my canvas before painting. I prefer to tack the unstretched canvas to the hard wall or the floor. I need the resistance of a hard surface. On the floor I am more at ease. I feel nearer, more a part of the painting, since this way I can walk around it, work from the four sides and literally be in the painting."[3] By resisting the convention of the easel as the structure of support for the composition of a painting, Pollock liberates painting from other structural conventions, not the least of which was the necessity that paint be applied on a canvas in order to draw a line. For what Pollock makes available in works like *Number 1A, 1948* is the possibility that a line no longer designate or trace a border, that it is "no longer the *edge* of anything."[4]

2. For reasons of copyright I am unable to reproduce the image of Pollock's painting here. To those unfamiliar with the work, please view it online at http://www.moma.org/collection/works/78699.

3. Pepe Karmel, ed., *Jackson Pollock: Interviews, Articles, and Reviews* (New York: Museum of Modern Art, 1999), 17.

4. Michael Fried, *Art and Objecthood: Essays and Reviews* (Chicago: University of Chicago Press, 1998), 106; Gilles Deleuze and

We might say this: Pollock's achievement is to interrupt the expectation that a line hold shape so as to make available an improper modality of line-potential previously unremarked. The line had always been just a line, useful for tracing edges, shapes, figures, or territories. But by affirming the availability of the line's drip, and by suspending the directedness of the brush stroke, Pollock makes available a new cosmology of line. To be sure, Pollock does not offer a new perspective on line; he advances a transubstantiation of line, exposing it as a process and not a substance. What is even more striking, when looking at a Pollock painting, is the sheer sense of wrongness that emerges from one's interface with it. There is nothing "right" about *Number 1A, 1948*; but there is nothing erroneous about it either. The work works. And it works because its line is improper.

To get a sense of the intensity of this gesture of impropriety, let us juxtapose it to Rousseau's discussion, at the beginning of the second part of the *Discourse on the Origins of Inequality*, of the utterance "this is mine."[5] With all its rhetorical flourishes, Rousseau accounts for this utterance as the historical, aesthetic, political, and metaphysical origin of inequality. That is, the invention and pronouncement of a linguistic line that permits the capacity to draw a line, parse a territory, put up a fence around a plot of land, and have that line and that fence count as belonging to someone (i.e., count as part of a person's part) *and* have all these intensities register as intelligible to others— such parts are, for Rousseau, the site (and source) of humanity's

---

Felix Guattari, *A Thousand Plateaus: Capitalism and Schizophrenia*, trans. Brian Massumi (Minneapolis: University of Minnesota Press, 1987), 298.

5. Jean-Jacques Rousseau, *The Discourses and Other Early Political Writings*, ed. Victor Gourevitch (Cambridge, U.K.: Cambridge University Press, 1997), 161.

fallenness. Inequality, for him, begins and ends with the techne of drawing a line on a flat surface and, subsequently, through speech and effort, to compose the shape of that line by figuring a territory and building a fence around it. The ontological precondition for property (including the propriety of self implicit in the "I" of "mine") is the existence of a geometrical line that designates shape: what we might call a property line, or the drawing of a lot.

Jackson Pollock's singular achievement—both aesthetic and political—is the disfiguration of the line; it is to free the line from the compellant must of having to draw shapes and thus purging it of its imperative of figuration. Within the history of modern aesthetics this gesture is tantamount to undermining the entirety of Western painting since the Renaissance—a paradigm shift, if you will, comparable to Einstein's theory of relativity and its undermining of Newtonian physics. Within political theory, this is tantamount to saying that territorial borders need no longer be drawn, that the surface of land is a smooth plateau on which the tracing of a line does not designate the existence of a territory; it is deterritorialization.[6] We might put the matter this way: Pollock's disfiguration of the line is an instance of impropriety in the face of an entire history of political thinking committed to (indeed, founded on) the line's capacity for bordering, of drawing and holding shapes (of nations, of principalities, of identities, of cultures, of class, of concepts, and so forth).

We define impropriety not as the absence of line, but as the nonnecessity of the line to rule. Impropriety exceeds the proper (i.e., *arche*/rule/*règle*), but is also that intensity that loosens the force of necessity *in* the proper. It is with these thoughts in mind that we affirm that democratic politics has always been aesthetic.

6. Deleuze and Guattari, *A Thousand Plateaus*, 172.

Thesis 10. On the Unusable

Aesthetic works are neither useful nor useless to politics. They are unusuable. The unusability of a work marks its stature as an aesthetic object. This is because aesthetic objects do not comply with the expectations of purposiveness. This also means that aesthetic objects are not knowable nor is their standing as political objects verifiable. The impropriety of an aesthetics of politics is its resistance to the epistemic demands of a politics of meaning.

IS IT POSSIBLE to affront aesthetic objects in terms other than their use value? In asking this question we want to mark a general tendency in contemporary cultural and political theory that regards the instrumentalization of aesthetics, through the elaboration of intricate epistemic matrices, for the purposes of a redemptive (and putatively progressive) politics.

One of the most available procedures for handling an aesthetics of politics regards the symptomatic analysis of appearances that unveils hidden structures of domination that such objects—and the institutions that generate them—are said to conceal. Here a commitment to various forms of emancipatory politics is wedded to an interpretive strategy equally committed to a hermeneutics of suspicion regarding the modes of expression (i.e., the knowledge claims) that such objects may convey. The result is a kind of policing function that regulates the relationship between forms of expression and structures of reference. Any object—whether written text, film, musical score, painting, photograph, and so forth—is said to exist within a fixed matrix of expression and reference: what aesthetic objects express is markedly different from what they represent, so that their obscured mode of world-relation betrays either an imposed or endured form of domination. The task of critical thinking vis-à-vis cultures of the spectacle is to treat the artifice of art as if it were a kind of veil intended to obscure the realities of coercion.

From this perspective the task of political critique is to unveil—or subtract—the artificiality of aesthetic objects in order to expose the concealed substrata of their referential functions. This formula of suspicion begins by suggesting that what an object seems to represent is different from its actual indexical properties and that in reality, that object imposes on the spectator certain structures of domination that she must wittingly or unwittingly endure. An aesthetically inflected mode of political and cultural theory must therefore deploy a searchlight of sorts that will illuminate and isolate what is symptomatic in these objects, reveal their structures of domination, and thus lift the veil of ignorance. In this manner political judgment secures emancipatory politics.

Such approaches to cultural criticism and the aesthetics of politics rely on an epistemic and instrumental correlation between the expressivity of objects and that to which they refer, a relation that also correlates to a concrete correspondence between perception and sensation. The result is a moral theory of the image that classifies aesthetic objects as intentional objects whose primary value is an instrumental one: the good or the bad image.

Let's call this general approach to the aesthetics of politics *the eschewal of aesthetics*. It is an eschewal of aesthetics because it denies us the possibility of relating to the world in any mode other than an instrumental one. Refusing the primordial convention that artifice is artificial, the eschewal of aesthetics admits that the only way to engage aesthetic objects is to treat them as epistemological objects whose purpose it is to make meaning. With the eschewal of aesthetics, the judge's objective becomes the delimitation of a human interest in the existence of aesthetic objects so as to determine a certain and verifiable knowledge of them; with such purposiveness as our ground we may attend to an object's indexical properties and thus administer its expressive functions. Politically, this means that the value of aesthetic objects is either useful because they promote a political and cultural agenda that we endorse, or useless because their demagogic properties veil the emancipatory potential of that same political and cultural agenda. In either case, and ironically so, the eschewal of aesthetics sanctions a commodification of culture to the extent that aesthetic objects become cultural commodities for the endorsement or rejection of certain specific political and theoretical interests.

The eschewal of aesthetics is iconoclastic in the Byzantine sense of the term. By wanting to unveil the artificiality of artifice in a work it endorses a mode of attending to aesthetic objects that dismantles the power of the image, or the intensity of immediacy in an appearance's advenience. More to the point, such an approach relies on a fundamental inequality between critic and audience. To endorse a hermeneutics of suspicion that sustains the position that aesthetic objects are collusive in their promotion of the commodification of culture means claiming access to a specialized, concrete knowledge about the substance of such objects, a specialized knowledge that is unavailable and perhaps even inaccessible to all. Here it is assumed that the spectator is passive and unable to see the spectacle of illusion that dictates a horizon of fixed ends; the role of the critic is thus that of the prophet who casts light on the mechanisms of misrecognition. With this posture of attention there exists only two potential subject positions: a passive and an active one, the audience and the critic.

But as we have seen, an aesthetics of politics that arises from an experience of aesthetic conviction can never satisfy the critic's "how do you know?" question. This is because an aesthetics of politics admits that the affirmations of the convictions it formulates are not subject to a knowing, nor are they available for verification via a line of intentionality. The *noli me tangere* of the advenience (Thesis 6) resists the normative, epistemic demand of the "how do you know?" From the position of an aesthetics of politics, the "how do you know?" question makes about as much sense as asking the epistemologist "can you show me metadata for the verification of the existence of your concept?"

What does it mean, then, to say that aesthetic objects are "unusable"?

It doesn't mean they are useless. Uselessness is the antithesis of use, to be sure. But unusability isolates a domain of value outside this logic of production and exchange. Aesthetic objects are unusable to the extent that they are not reducible to an instrumental logic that guarantees the use/uselessness dialectic as the basis for political and aesthetic critique. In other words, aesthetic objects are not purposive, though they invite creative modes of handling.

To say this is to suggest that the principle of unusability is grounded in a classical aesthetic thesis that sustains the idea that aesthetic objects—in order to count as aesthetic—are not reducible to their qualities. This means—crucially—that aesthetic objects *are not* things "for us." This is what Kant meant

when he forwarded the radical democratic thesis of "disinterest" by affirming that there can be no rules to determine
the beauty of an object because the object is exempt from—
that is, *unusable to*—the logic of interest.[1] Oddly enough this
is the most sublime and un-Kantian moment in all of Kant's
writings—and, in fact, it is the moment when Kant is closest
to David Hume. And there is no doubt that Kant himself may
have realized this, which helps explain his subsequent retreat
in affirming the beautiful as a symbol of the moral. For Kant,
the radical heteronomy of the *unusability* of aesthetic objects
was difficult to bear—his critical system could not hold it up.
Thus he had to reinstate a structure of interest for the aesthetic
by aligning it with the moral.

But the dispensation of interest thesis—articulated by Hume
and partly sustained by Kant—has never gone away, and it is at
the heart of the unusability of aesthetic objects for politics: *The
principle of unusability allows us to play with the idea that the
human, natural, and social sciences need not be exclusively committed to the symbolic interpretation of meaning or the production of understanding.* Meaning and understanding are always
for someone or *for* something; they always have a use value, or
an interest. This is why Kant had to invoke analogy to suture
the tear of the aesthetic caesura that inserted a radical heteronomy into his critical system.

Now, none of this implies that we do not, or ought not, make
critical judgments that assert the meaning of things: that's
precisely the task of critical thinking, and the task of judgment. But theory—the fabulation of the virtuality of worlds—
and criticism—the asseveration of our beliefs about a thing's

1. Immanuel Kant, *Critique of the Power of Judgment*, trans. Paul
Guyer and Eric Matthews (Cambridge, U.K.: Cambridge University
Press, 2000).

workings—are two distinct activities. What we point to in drawing this blurred relation between theory and criticism, then, is the possibility of thinking the value and objecthood of things in and of themselves, without having to bear the weight of epistemic validation.

The problem of aesthetic experience is one of having to come to terms with the unusability of aesthetic value in the face of its intensity and inexhaustibility. An aesthetic experience is one in which one has a sensation of incisive conviction regarding the presentness of an object, despite the fact that there is no source or site of evidence that will count as necessary or sufficient to determining the validity of that incision. There is a political force to this aesthetic insight that says that with the dispensation of necessity we unleash the intensity of the otherwise. Anything whatever might happen otherwise, and thus everything is also otherwise thinkable, otherwise doable. What an aesthetics of politics affords, ultimately, is a dispensing with the consequentialism of necessity. In this way we admit of the unusability of aesthetic objects for politics. To do so means to place the expectations of signification at the level of all other criteria, dispensing with their necessity, and acknowledging that the content of things is an aspect of objects, but one aspect among many.

The frictions that adveniences procure bespeak a resistance to the instrumental expectations of the epistemic. I take this to be the full force of Roland Barthes's admonition that the *punctum* does not enlist an account of any specific kernel of knowledge, but the recounting of an event of sensorial interface with the allure of things. When Barthes advises that he will remonstrate with his moods and not justify them, he resists the epistemic demands of verification for experience; as does Jean-Luc Godard when he shows on a blackboard in a frame of *Le Vent D'Est* (1970) this aphorism: "Ce n'est *pas* une *image juste*, c'est

juste une *image*" ("It is not a just image; it is just an image");
and as does Stanley Cavell when he affirms that "I can't tell
you how I know"[2] that my relating one aspect to another is an
actual relation, however virtual it might be. It's just a fact of
aesthetic experience: we simply can't verify our convictions of
the power of a work of art by referencing it to a schema of legit-
imacy that underwrites our political and knowledge interests.
But that doesn't mean that we are unaware of the experience,
nor does it mean that we should not tend to the experience,
that we should not be/hold it, that it doesn't matter because
it is not politically useful, and that we ought not remark on a
remarkable sensation. Quite to the contrary, the advenience of
aesthetic experience is a remarkable political fact.

2. Cavell, *Claim of Reason*, 358.

Coda

What we remonstrate with these ten theses is nothing less than the possibility of a politics of appearances that disposes a curatorial regard for the experience of attending to a world that one remarks on for the first time, despite the fact that such a world might have always been apparent. And that is perhaps the point: what we experience in the advenience is that there is a world that appears, and that the appearance of the world is something that warrants attending to in and of itself. The entirely contingent event of sensation rooted in nothing other than the ingression of an advenience carries with it the potential to form attachments and detachments with those peoples, objects, and elements that appear in everyday life. Therein lies an aesthetics of politics: a partaking in the life of sensation that renders available those luminosities previously held insensible.

Further Writings

Panagia, Davide. "Aesthetics and Politics." In *Encyclopedia of Political Thought*, edited by Michael T. Gibbons, Diana Coole, Elisabeth Ellis, and Kennan Ferguson, 17–23. Malden, Mass.: Wiley-Blackwell, 2014.

——. "Blankets, Screens, and Projections: On Stanley Cavell's Aesthetics of Politics." In *The Aesthetic Turn in Political Theory*, edited by Nikolas Kompridis, 229–63. London: Continuum Press, 2014.

——. "Cinéma vérité and the Ontology of Cinema: A Reply to Roy Germano." *Perspectives on Politics* 12, no. 3 (2014): 688–90.

——. "Exposures and Projections: Simon Critchley's Ethics of Appearances." In *Politics of Religion / Religion of Politics*, edited by Alistair Welchman, 99–115. New York: Springer, 2014.

——. "Films Blancs: Luminosity in the Films of Michael Mann." *Film-Philosophy* 19 (2015): http://www.film-philosophy.com/index.php/f-p/article/view/963.

——. "Food as Fuel and an Ethics of Appearances." *Theory and Event* 12, no. 2 (2009): https://muse.jhu.edu/article/269992.

——. "Influence and Entanglement of Mediatic Diffusion with Technology." *Scienza e Tecnica: Rivista di informazione della societa' Italiana per il progresso delle scienze* 76 (2014): 521–22.

——. "The Monstrous Art of Pop." *Gaga Stigmata*, September 29, 2010: http://gagajournal.blogspot.com/2010/09/monstrous-art-of-pop.html.

——. "The Notion of Pantry: A Speculative Defense of Unuse in the Humanities." *World Picture Journal* 6 (Fall 2011): http://www.worldpicturejournal.com/WP_6/Panagia.html.

———. "A Politics of Appearances." *Hannah Arendt Center,* November 26, 2012: http://www.hannaharendtcenter.org/a-politics-of -appearances/.

———. "A Theory of Aspects: Media Participation in Political Theory." *New Literary History* 45, no. 4 (2014): 527–48.

Davide Panagia is associate professor of political science at UCLA. His books include *The Poetics of Political Thinking*; *The Political Life of Sensation*; and *Impressions of Hume: Cinematic Thinking and the Politics of Discontinuity*.